Dogs Working for People

By Joanna Foster / Photographs by James L. Stanfield

Books for Young Explorers

NATIONAL GEOGRAPHIC SOCIETY

What's out there?
Pan finds this world full of strange sounds,
good smells, and wonderful things to chew.

GOLDEN RETRIEVER

There is also her master, David.
When Pan is a little older, David teaches her
to go out for a boat bumper and bring it back.
That's easy for Pan. She's a born retriever.

GOLDEN RETRIEVER

5

Rogue is a retriever too.
Splash! Into the water he plunges, when his master says, "Fetch!"
A hunting dog like this is trained not to bite the duck
he retrieves but to bring it back carefully.

LABRADOR RETRIEVER

Where are those birds?
Now Ringo smells them!
His whole body stiffens.
His nose points straight to the place
where the birds are hiding.
Ringo won't move or make a sound
until his master gives him a command.

Hunting was one of the first kinds of work
dogs ever did for men.
Today, along with hunting, there are many
other ways dogs are working for people.

Dingo is an expert at moving stubborn cows.
Run up. Nip her on the heel. Duck down quick.
Nip her again if she doesn't keep going.
This kind of dog, called a "heeler," is quick to learn
what a rancher wants him to do.

AUSTRALIAN CATTLE DOG

BORDER COLLIE

Keep moving. Step along there.
Ginger's job is to help the shepherd move all these sheep to a new pasture.

Get in line, sheep. You all need to be sheared.
Cubby jumps on top of their woolly backs.
On command from his master, he directs them through the chute,
nipping an ear now and then to keep them moving.

BORDER COLLIE

AFGHAN HOUND

"Stand still! Hold your head up!"
Each person urges his dog to show off, hoping to win
a blue ribbon.
Big dogs, little dogs, thousands of dogs of every size and shape
were brought to this big dog show.
And the little Maltese won the top prize.

SPRINGER SPANIEL, BELGIAN SHEEPDOG, WEIMARANER

POODLES

MALTESE

GERMAN SHEPHERDS

Many dogs go to school to learn obedience,
but these dogs go to a special school.
As Seeing Eye dogs, each learns to guide a master who is blind.

The special harness lets the man quickly feel when his dog wants
to steer him away from danger.

GREYHOUND

Running, running as fast as you can.
That's what counts for a greyhound like Tresca.
She wears a racing muzzle on her mouth and a white blanket on her back.
Streaking around the track is great!

BLOODHOUND

Most dogs have a keen sense of smell.
They use their noses as people use their eyes.
Apples, a bloodhound puppy, is learning to use her nose
to search for people and rescue them when they're lost in the woods.

"O.K. Peley, find him!"
That's the signal
to follow the scent.
There and there.

BLOODHOUND

24

Peley's found you!
This gentle dog
won't jump or bark,
but he is happy
when he finds
the person
he's searching for.

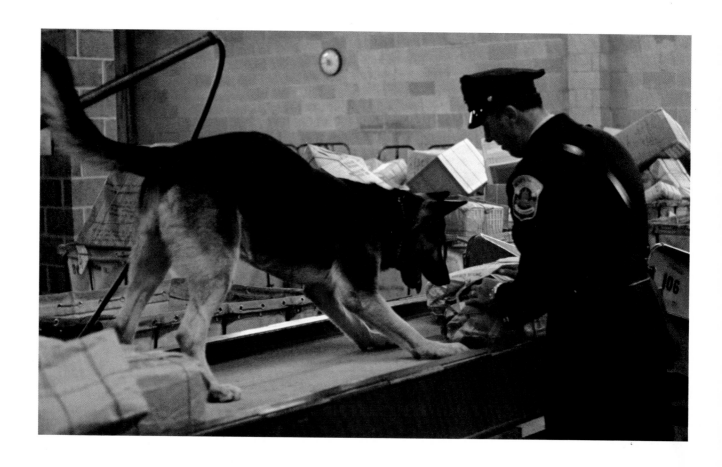

Dutch gets his praise for sniffing out illegal drugs
that are hidden in packages. Here, this one!
This package has it!

Ruff! Ruff!
There's that smell! Dynamite!
Lucky has been trained to bark when he finds that special smell,
so that he can help the policemen on the bomb squad.

GERMAN SHEPHERD

GERMAN SHEPHERD

Shane is always on the alert,
watching, listening.
He has been taught what to do
and how to act
as a police dog.
He is ready for trouble,
but he will only attack
when there is danger.

28

Listen! Where is that noise?
Is there a burglar hiding behind one of the counters?
If there is, Peter will find him.

Every night, after the store closes, this guard dog
and others like him go on patrol.
A dog can hear and smell much better than a person,
and Peter can hear sounds that his handler can't.

DOBERMAN PINSCHER

"Five, four, three, two, one—Go!"
With a wild yelping, this team of Huskies bounds ahead,
off on a fifteen-mile sled dog race.

SIBERIAN HUSKIES

Dog teams and sleds once pulled heavy loads for the Eskimos. Now, dogs like Kiska and her granddaughter Nikki are trained and raced on weekends by children as well as their parents.

WIRE FOX TERRIER

A spotlight on
the center ring.
A burst of music.
And the circus dogs
begin their tricks.
Spot leaps
from his high ladder,
while Tony balances
on his scooter.
Jack rides the pony
and Kropki plays
with the clowns.

WIRE FOX TERRIER

SMOOTH FOX TERRIER

MINIATURE SCHNAUZER

Lassie has been a television star for a long time.
She watches her trainer Rudd, the man in the blue shirt, for directions.
"Lassie come. Easy now."
Rudd is telling her to come to the boy and the hurt dog.
In this story Lassie has just found them and must go for help.

GERMAN SHEPHERD AND COLLIE

39

"Good dog! That's a good dog!"
Lassie is always eager to hear these words.
All dogs need praise for the things they learn
and the work they do well.

COLLIE